Park News

42 PAGES

NEWS OFFICE
202 Broad Street

ST 17, 1951   DAILY, TEN CENTS

Auto Dealerships See Super Summer

Sales Higher Throughout County

By MICHAEL DULY, JR.

SINESS DISTRICT — "This is the kind of season you hope for but don't always get." says Rich Nubbins, senior salesman at Nubbins Studebaker. "I chalk up our success a reliable, well-built product, backed up by expert sales and service." Others interwed for this piece said it was simply a matter of new, dazzling models in the showoms across town. According to longtime resident Jane Durkin, "My husband chose car, but I got to pick the color. It was hard, they're all so beautiful!" She chose red. Used car dealerships also saw sizeable gains during the summer months. John Dryer OK Used Cars set a personal sales record for the month of July. "I expected sales to off, simply because so many residents are out at the lake for the summer." Asked out his August numbers so far, Dryer smiled broadly and said simply, "No complaints atsoever." Even Ed's Car Wash added two towel men to keep up with demand. Says

See Auto Sales, Pg B5

Orbit Ice Cream Celebrates 10th Year

By HELEN LINDSTROM

GIN PARK VILLAGE — Nevermind that it's located on Bank St., the outer reaches

GROVE STREET EXTENSION GETS GO-AHEAD FOR WEST SIDE

Town Council Unanimously Approves New Measure

By P.J. DONAHUE

BACKBONE RD. — For the twelve members of Elgin Park's Town Council, it was not a hard decision to make. Indeed, residents of Elgin Park's far West Side have been appearing at monthly community board meetings in droves to lobby for an extension of Grove Street. "The area has so much potential, but it can only be reached from one direction, and as a result most townspeople have trouble finding it." So says West Side resident John Montgomery. "Many might be surprised to know the far West Side has the largest natural Oak arbor in the state, or that it has the largest concentration of tributaries flowing from the Ohio River." Apart

Elgin Park Student Wins Young Inventor Award

PRAISES TEACHERS IN SPEECH

By NED TURTLETAUB

ELGIN PARK HIGH — Peter Novesky was a born tinkerer. As his mother recalls, "He once disassembled the very crib we put him in. We didn't leave the room but for a minute, and when we returned, he had removed every last slat from the sides of that crib and was beginning to fashion them into a ladder so as to escape."

While such a tall-tale is hard to verify, and may have been embellished over the years by proud parents, there is no doubting Peter's natural abilities when it comes to feats of engineering and creativity. A member of Elgin Park's Science Society from the age of ten, he has been producing a steady stream of clever contraptions for years: a key ring that emits a beeping sound should you misplace it; a stick-less popsicle; a bicycle designed specifically for delivering newspapers (*hint:* you can steer it using only one hand).

The Young Inventor Award—presented every two years by the Science Society—is awarded based not on one particular invention; but is instead given to an inventor under the age of eighteen who shows "a consistent bent of mind towards the creation of the new." While Novesky is not the youngest Society member to win the award (that distinction belongs to thirteen-year-old Chip Barnes, in 1947), he does hold the most patents on record for

See Young Inventor, Pg B10

"Elgin Park Cookbook" Soliciting Contributions

The Elgin Park Ladies Auxiliary is soliciting recipes for their upcoming *Elgin Park Cookbook*. Residents are encouraged to include a short description of why they enjoy the recipe, such as "family favorite" or "a new twist on an old standby." Recipes should be typed or neatly handwritten, and mailed to: *Cookbook*, P.O. Box 109

MICHAEL PAUL SMITH / ELGIN PARK NEWS

Borden's To Offer Expanded Delivery

By MICHAEL NUSSBAUM

MAIN STREET — Every Elgin Park resident is accustomed to the sight of Borden's unique snub-nosed delivery vans scooting along Main Street, but starting in September they may be able to see those same delivery vans idling in their own driveways. Long a staple of restaurants and soda fountains town-wide, Borden's has announced that they will begin home delivery of their products in October. According to Jim McHugh, Borden's chief customer sales representative, the dairy producer intends on becoming as familiar to Elgin Park residents as their mail man or meter maid. "We are known for the freshness of our products. By adding home delivery, we can ensure our customers

See Home Delivery, Pg A7

ELGIN PARK

ELGIN

PARK

AN IDEAL AMERICAN TOWN · *by* · MICHAEL PAUL SMITH ·

To my Mother and Father,

who provided me with a safe and loving childhood.

For my sons, Spencer and Dylan.

And to Henry, *Mannaggia!*

© Prestel Verlag, Munich · London · New York 2011
All photography © Michael Paul Smith 2011

Front cover: *Elgin Main Street 1951*
Endpapers and map by Mark Melnick

Prestel Verlag, Munich
A member of Verlagsgruppe Random House GmbH

PRESTEL VERLAG
Neumarkter Strasse 28 · 81673 Munich
Tel. +49 (0)89 24 29 08-300 · Fax +49 (0)89 24 29 08-335

www.prestel.de

PRESTEL PUBLISHING LTD.
4 Bloomsbury Place · London WC1A 2QA
Tel. +44 (0)20 7323-5004 · Fax +44 (0)20 7636-8004

PRESTEL PUBLISHING
900 Broadway, Suite 603 · New York, NY 10003
Tel. +1 (212) 995-2720 · Fax +1 (212) 995-2733

www.prestel.com

Library of Congress Control Number: 2010939233
British Library Cataloguing-in-Publication Data: a catalogue record for this book
is available from the British Library; Deutsche Nationalbibliothek holds a record of this publication
in the Deutsche Nationalbibliografie; detailed bibliographical data can be found under:
http://dnb.d-nb.de

Prestel books are available worldwide. Please contact your nearest bookseller or one of
the above addresses for information concerning your local distributor.

EDITORIAL DIRECTION: Christopher Lyon · EDITORIAL ASSISTANCE: Ryan Newbanks
PRODUCTION: The Production Department · DESIGN AND LAYOUT: Mark Melnick
COLOR SEPARATIONS: Robert J. Hennessey · PRINTING AND BINDING: Midas Printing, China

Printed on 170gsm Lumi FSC matte

ISBN 978-3-7913-4548-2

Contents

WELCOME TO

ELGIN PARK

"TAKE YOUR TIME"

Michael Paul Smith may be aware of contemporary culture, but his heart lives in the past. Inspired by Sewickley, Pennsylvania, his hometown in the 1940s and '50s, Smith has worked for years to create the imaginary Elgin Park. He not only remembers streets, buildings, cars, and everyday products from his childhood but, more significantly, continues to live in accordance with values held by his parents and neighbors: humility in place of hubris, generosity rather than greed, passion instead of profit.

JUST WASHED

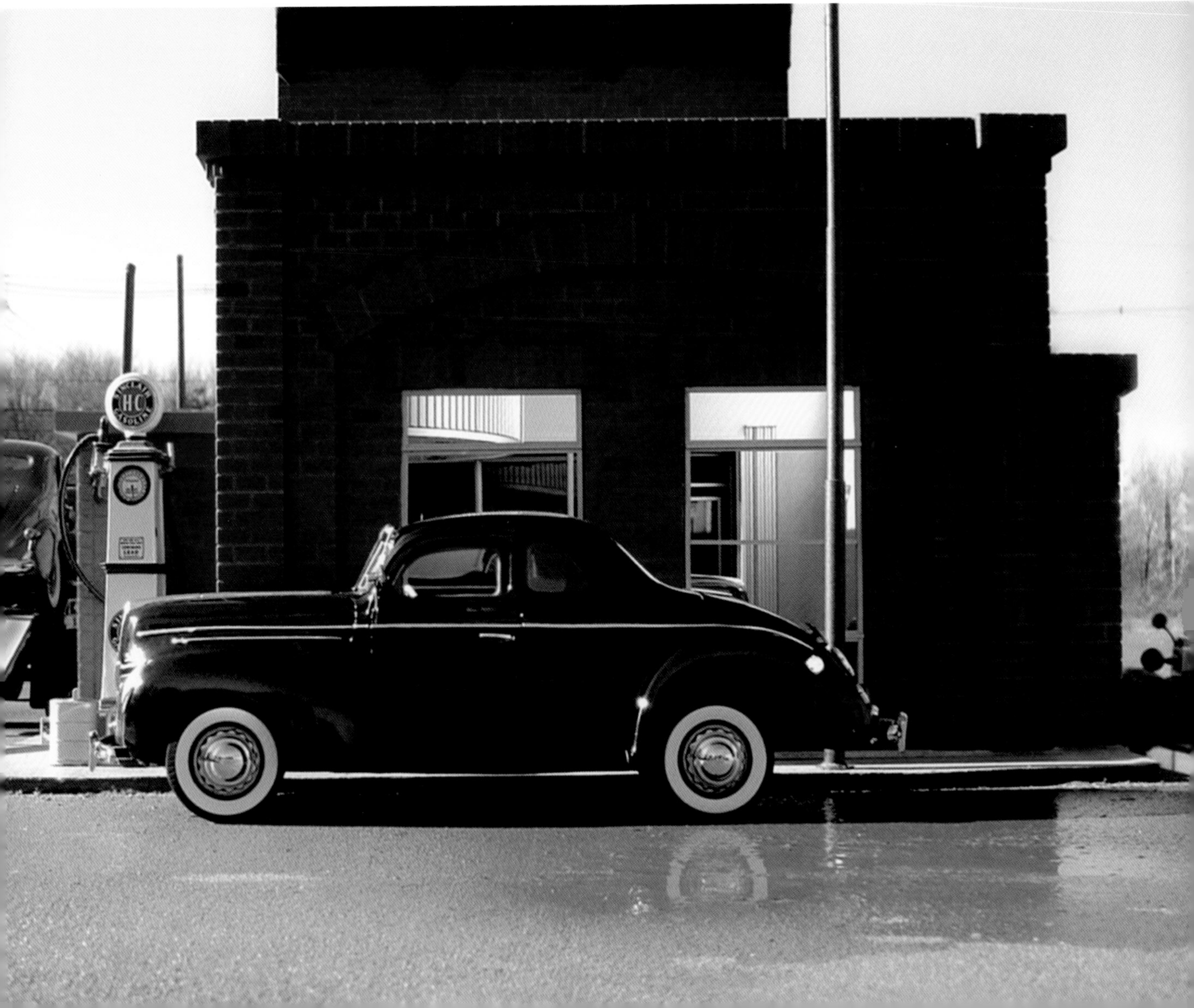

Now, thanks to the internet, Elgin Park has touched the hearts of millions of people all over the world—even twenty-somethings who have no personal connection to the era beyond the photographs on their grandmother's mantel or images from black-and-white television reruns. Smith's professional experience as an illustrator, art director, interior painter, museum display- designer, and architectural model-maker prepared him to create Elgin Park, but his love affair with models goes back fifty years:

> I have always been fascinated with models and miniatures. Even in grade school I made buildings out of cigar boxes and put interiors in them. That was also true of car, truck, and train models. I'd put wheels on shoeboxes and cut out windows. I discovered plastic car kits in the late '50s, but it was the AMT Chevy Impala kit I received for my 12th birthday that was the defining moment for me. Speed up to the 1980s when diecast cars started to appear, and it was all downhill for me. I was always fond of the cars by independent automakers that filled my neighborhood in the '50s. In my photos I try to conjure up the feeling that not every car was a Ford or Chevy. The independent makes were so unique looking. Even as a kid I knew that.
>
> These vehicles are my only vice. Three hundred 1/24th-scale [one-quarter inch equals one foot] diecasts sitting on a shelf might look impressive, but there was something sad about that. They needed to be put in context, and a scale building of some sort would help bring some life to them. A gas station seemed a logical choice because it was timeless and iconic. I found a partially destroyed commercial G-scale structure in the trash and decided to fix it up and add an interior. Most important, it had to be as good as the diecast cars. So I put a huge effort into getting the details correct—went online to find photos of older neighborhood gas stations from the '40s and '50s. When it was completed, I placed some cars around it and took some photographs. That was an "Aha!" moment for me, and it was only

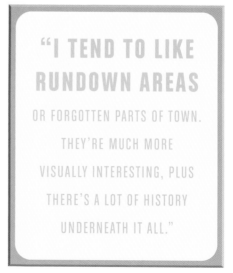

"I TEND TO LIKE RUNDOWN AREAS OR FORGOTTEN PARTS OF TOWN. THEY'RE MUCH MORE VISUALLY INTERESTING, PLUS THERE'S A LOT OF HISTORY UNDERNEATH IT ALL."

a matter of time before I started to design and make my own structures. Ultimately I ended up with fifteen buildings.

With the success of that first project, I started thinking about what kind of neighborhood this gas station would be in and what those structures should look like. I tend to like rundown areas or forgotten parts of town. They're much more visually interesting, plus there's a lot of history underneath it all.

At the start Smith wanted to recreate Sewickley as accurately as possible; he photographed every commercial structure in town. "That was the geek in me!" he admits. But as he became more involved as an artist, Smith realized that his scenes would have greater emotional impact if the structures were not tied to a specific location and time. After all, Sewickley was just one incarnation of mid-century small-town America—still to be discovered on two-lane roads in many parts of the country. It became his goal to capture, as he puts it, "the mood of an era," which replaces absolute verisimilitude with gut-level manipulation of lighting, suggestion of seasons, hints of details lodged in memory, and a believable age-range of vehicles that might have appeared simultaneously in front of a given home or storefront.

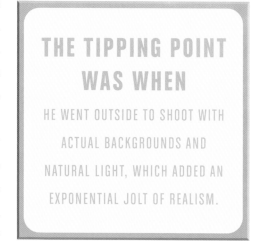

THE TIPPING POINT WAS WHEN HE WENT OUTSIDE TO SHOOT WITH ACTUAL BACKGROUNDS AND NATURAL LIGHT, WHICH ADDED AN EXPONENTIAL JOLT OF REALISM.

Smith's earlier photographs have a slightly cleaner, more staged feeling than those he has created more recently. As time went on, he became more adventurous and sprinkled dirt and dust on some surfaces, which helped to add a nitty-gritty element. But the tipping point was when he went outside to shoot with actual backgrounds and natural light, which added an exponential jolt of realism. It wasn't long before he was taking dramatic night shots with water and fog.

Part of Smith's artistry lies in the fact that the specifics are there, but not too many of them. This sensitivity stems from Smith's employment over an 18-year period as a model-builder in an architectural firm. As he explains,

The brain/eye/emotions will fill in the details, even when there is a minimum of information available. You can have too much information, and when that happens, you end up with a literal representation of something and very little room for personal interpretation. The more the viewer can project him or herself into something, the more powerful it becomes. For me, it's all about focusing on the emotional gesture—the combination of aesthetic elements that creates for viewers the emotional feeling that I had while building the models and setting up the shots. It's about story, not about buildings, and not even about the cars, much as I love them.

CASUAL VIEWERS MIGHT NOT NOTICE HIS BUILDINGS' INTERIORS, WHICH ARE COMPLETE AND REFLECT ACCURATELY THE PERIOD DEPICTED.

Working on Elgin Park, Smith became particularly sensitive to details that distract from the larger scene, like gravel that isn't perfectly to scale, or colors in shades that aren't true to the time of day, or surfaces without reflections. Again, this isn't a matter of precisely replicating reality. "Just because something is, let's say, red," he notes, "it can be painted a different version of red, or you can imply that it's red. The brain does some wonderful gymnastics to make the world coherent."

"When looking at old photos," Smith points out, "you'll notice that telephone poles lean, buildings are cobbled together, cars are not parked neatly, and there's a layer of 'time passed' over everything. That is the look I go for." He adds more about his creative process:

There are a few things about making models and photographing them that are peak experiences. First is doing research and coming up with an era that would be interesting. Studying old photographs inspires me. Not the posed ones, but the snap shots and "outtakes." Mostly they are insignificant moments in time that have been captured and trigger very old memories. You know how certain smells can bring your past back? I've found that to be true in the visual world, too.

From there it's creating a look that suggests time has passed through the buildings and scene. There are rarely completely new buildings all lined up in a row. If you look

around, you will notice buildings have been added on to; streets have been repaved; vehicles are not all brand new. It's those kinds of details that add subtle layers to any given scene. That's the level where magic comes into play.

Each building takes about four weeks to research and construct. Most are made from Gatorboard—a 3/16-inch foam sandwiched between two pieces of resin-coated paper—a board that is lightweight and durable and can be cut with a knife. Basswood is the artist's wood of choice because its tight grain is the proper scale. Most of the exterior details are assembled using styrene plastic and plexiglas (which comes in many translucent period colors). He uses commercial household spray paint in cans, preferably matte or flat finish.

Smith paints bricks and mortar by hand, adding weathering and age. Winter is suggested by baking-soda snow (which sticks to tires with the addition of water); adding a little soap to water makes the "rain" not bead up on the street. To enhance believability, he made a miniature broom and snow shovel, which leave realistic tracks and characteristic patterns—all to scale. Smith makes most such objects himself, though he will use a purchased item if it fits the need. "I'm especially proud of the push mower and washing machine I made," he says, "and also the porch glider and matching chair." In his diner interior, many details are created using found objects—rarely recognizable because they appear at a different scale. His secret? "What I need is usually in the room I'm in."

A POWERFUL PERSONAL SYMBOL TO THE ARTIST, THE BUNGALOW FEATURED IN MANY PHOTOS TOOK LONGER TO CONSTRUCT BECAUSE IT IS COMPLETELY FURNISHED.

Casual viewers might not notice his buildings' interiors, which are complete and reflect accurately the period depicted, including printed linoleum patterns on floors, chrome counters, bread awaiting purchase, and advertisements on the walls. Outside are billboards of the era. There is a true-to-period box in the garbage truck. In the shoe store, there are more than 100 individual boxes (not labeled with size and color!). The TV repair shop has parts of dismantled sets strewn about.

A powerful personal symbol to the artist, the bungalow featured in many photos took longer to construct because it is completely furnished with carpets, sheets on the bed, and canisters in the kitchen. There's even a fold-down ironing board and a glider on the front porch that actually rocks, though as Smith adds defensively, "If it's any consolation, the doors and windows don't open."

When photographing indoors, scenes are generally illuminated by a bare 40- or 60-watt bulb suspended overhead or from the side. Single white Christmas-tree bulbs or battery-powered LEDs light building interiors. The outdoor details are simple: rain is water from the sink; gutter dirt is detritus from the vacuum cleaner bag. Other modelers appreciate Smith's time investment and commitment. As one blogger noted, "The models take days or months to build, defying our culture's insistence on instant gratification. They were not built with an eye to making money—another surprise in today's world."

Once he has mocked up the scene and examined it from all angles, Smith often goes outside to look for a suitable location for the shoot—ideally a field or parking lot with about a

block's worth of unobstructed view so that the background will be in scale with the model, which is balanced on a folding table in the foreground.

When the shooting starts, the magic begins, governed by emotions, intuition, and remembering not to try too hard. "When photographing a scene," Smith says, "I always have

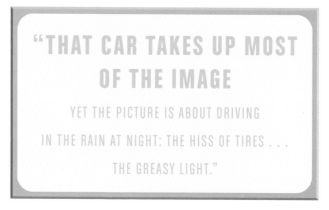

"THAT CAR TAKES UP MOST OF THE IMAGE

YET THE PICTURE IS ABOUT DRIVING IN THE RAIN AT NIGHT: THE HISS OF TIRES . . . THE GREASY LIGHT."

the viewer in mind because I want him or her to be able to emotionally access the finished image. If there is too much of my own personal baggage, then the photo just becomes a curiosity. There's a real balancing act going on in my head during a shoot. What I learned early on when taking these photographs is that it's not about the individual cars or buildings. Even if there's a single car in the shot, it shouldn't say 'Hey, look at me!'"

An example is the photo of the Mercury Turnpike Cruiser outside the White Castle restaurant. "That car takes up most of the image," Smith notes, "yet the picture is about driving in

LATE NIGHT *Snack*

Crestliner BY THE TRACKS

the rain late at night: the hiss of the tires of passing cars on a wet street, the greasy light from the building's interior that we all know so well when we grab a late meal while on the road. All of it is very personal to me, yet it's familiar to everyone else, but for different reasons."

A shoot lasts about an hour, with about 20 to 30 photos, of which there are, on average, a couple of good shots. Because the creative process continues well beyond model-building and placement of vehicles, some of the photos are the result of pure serendipity:

> I remember the day it occurred to me that I could drive some of my models to Pittsburgh and do a week-long photo shoot. I couldn't believe I never thought of it before. My first destination was the railroad tracks near the Sewickley Bridge. I got there at eight o'clock in the morning and set up the model base on the roof of the rented car. I needed the height to line up the set with the train tracks. And then the Universe sent along a freight train as I was taking pictures. It was a perfect moment!

This outdoor artistry sometimes requires skill at human relations: some people have a hard time understanding what Smith is doing. (For this reason, he always carries photos of his work.) A policeman might show up and give him "the look." He asks permission from the surrounding homeowners, even if their house will be a blur in the background. Sometimes they don't agree or change their minds, but Smith's unassuming and congenial manner generally convinces them.

Perhaps the most surprising aspect of the work is that Smith shoots with a six-megapixel $75 Sony Cyber-Shot. Smith says that his three-megapixel camera took even better "vintage" photos because older point-and-shoot camera lenses caused a mild blur—a blur that holds the key to the look of the past, adding emotional distance and mystery.

Given how human and personal these images feel—some viewers swear that they see blurry figures driving some of the cars—it is remarkable that they contain no people. From the beginning, Smith believed that including figures would dis-

> "I GOT THERE AT EIGHT O'CLOCK IN THE MORNING AND SET UP THE MODEL . . . AND THEN THE UNIVERSE SENT ALONG A FREIGHT TRAIN AS I WAS TAKING PICTURES."

tract viewers from imagining their own narratives. "When you start to place your own thoughts into the picture, it becomes more personal," he says. "Memories or stories you've heard over the years begin to fill in the blanks. It all becomes dreamlike. And that's when the fun begins."

First-time viewers assume that the images must be created in Photoshop, but they are not. Smith uses Photoshop only for occasional adjustment of color to give an image more of a "period" look, making it black-and-white, sepia-toned, or giving the image the appearance of Kodachrome slide film. He also admits to having once used Photoshop to remove an insect from an outdoor shot.

Given the simplicity and economy of his low-tech equipment, it is all the more amazing that Smith's work achieved recognition via high-tech viral spread on the internet. In addition to tallying over 23 million viewers on Flickr and being mentioned on over 200 blogs, Smith's artwork has been featured in The New York Times, The Times of London, and even the Russian edition of Automobile Quarterly. He's been on all three of the nation's top television networks. Suddenly this modest man working at a kitchen table and using a point-and-shoot camera has found his photographs featured by the Craftsmanship Museum in Vista, California. He's currently preparing for a group exhibition that will be mounted in June 2011 at the Museum of Arts and Design in New York City that will explore the reality of dioramas.

The international appeal of Elgin Park suggests the powerful effects that the photographs have on the psyche of viewers—some of whom have even Photoshopped themselves into the photographs in period dress, creating a virtual community. As Smith notes, even the name Elgin Park, which came to him out of nowhere, conjures up the essence of "small town": stability, isolation but not desolation, family and unlocked doors. In email or comments posted online, visitors speak of longing for home. "Many people have written that they feel a deeper story going on in my work," he says. "One wrote, 'I am crying; I am crying.' It's about childhood, family, longing, happiness, love, and sadness—the same emotions that flow in when we bring a box of our own dusty photos down from the attic."

Reading and responding to such comments brings Smith himself to tears. Smith remembers the day he realized what an effect his work was having: "A woman from England wrote to me and said 'I'll be in the States and I want to visit Elgin Park.' I let her down gently. The woman never wrote back. I think I broke her heart."   —GAIL K. ELLISON

ELGIN PARK

Elgin Park

NOTABLE DESTINATIONS

A Kenmore

B R. C. Binkmeister Office

C Gibson Florist

D Superette

E The Elgin Theater

F Studebaker Dealership

G Wash & Dry Laundromat

H Vivian's

I Rainbow Bar

J Hegner's Paint

K White Tower Restaurant

L Service Station

M Tip-Top Toys

N Orbit Ice Cream

O OK Used Cars

P Elgin Park Research Center

Q Dink's Speed Shop

R Barber Shop

KOSCS WAY

BOUNDARY ST.

RUTH AVE.

BEAVER CT.

THORN ST.

WALSH LANE

SIDNEY ST.

MCDONALD ST.

SUNSET LANE

N

Scale 1:250,000

5   0   5   10

OHIO RIVER

Dreamtime PARKING LOT

Saturday NIGHT 1933

TORNADO

Christmas 1946

WESTERN PENNA. – WINTER 1946

WINTER 1946

First SNOW OF THE SEASON

POWER OUTAGE

GARAGE WITH *Buick*

Down BY FERRIS STREET

Elgin CAR SALES

Homage TO CHARLES CUSHMAN

Parking BEHIND THE DINER

Superette

Elgin THEATER – MAIN STREET

J&L STEEL – NIGHT GLOW

Flat-Bed TRUCK 1940

AFTER THE RAIN

CLOSING TIME

WORKING LATE

STUDEBAKER SHOWROOM

ROOFTOP VIEW

NO PARKING FROM HERE TO CORNER

ACROSS THE TRAIN TRACKS

MR. ETWOOD'S YELLOW *Cadillac*

10 P.M.

JULY 4TH, 1951

White TOWER PARKING LOT

Sunday, MEDFORD SQUARE 1955

LOCAL BURGER JOINT

Service DEPARTMENT 1964

VIEW FROM THE *Passenger's* WINDOW

LAST WASH

COLD MERCURY

WASH & DRY

AFTER THE *Holidays*

NEW YEAR'S DAY SNOWFALL

Hegner's HARDWARE STORE

BIG BLACK *Chevy*

A BRIGHT, COLD, EARLY SPRING DAY

TWO TONE '59 *El Camino*

ELGIN PARK

VISTA-VISION *Bungalow*

Train WHISTLE BLOWING

THE FAMILY'S NEW '55

LATE AFTERNOON

VISTA-VISION *Lincoln*

THE *Best* STREET IN TOWN

Woodie WITH TRAILER

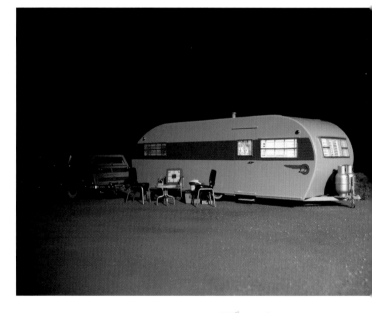

Trailer BY NIGHT

FAMILY VACATION

Memories OF SEWICKLEY

MR. VOIGHT'S '49 *Oldsmobile*

Thompson BEACH PARKING LOT

Corner TOY STORE

Matinee AT THE ELGIN

THE NEIGHBORS' BACKYARD

KEN'S NEW WHITE-WALL TIRES

Laundry AND BARBER SHOP

USED CAR LOT AT NIGHT

Burger JOINT IN THE RAIN

LAST CALL

LATE NIGHT LAUNDROMAT REPAIR

THE OLD ELGIN 1962

THE DEPOT PARKING LOT

EARLY EVENING

Dealership

NEW IN THE SHOWROOM 1960

WHILE OTHERS SLEEP

PARKING IN THE ALLEY

PIGEON'S-EYE VIEW

ORBIT ICE CREAM 1959

USED CARS 1961

Research PARKING LOT 1958

First OFF THE CAR CARRIER

Ready FOR THE WEEKEND

1964 COMMUTER TRAIN PARKING LOT

GARBAGE TRUCK

LEAVING THE ENGINE *Running*

NORTH OF ELGIN PARK

About the Artist & Author

MICHAEL PAUL SMITH lives in Winchester, Massachusetts. Educated at The School of the Worcester Art Museum and the University of Massachusetts, he has been an art director, illustrator of textbooks, wallpaper hanger, interior house painter, and museum display designer. He works part-time as a model maker and archivist for a Boston architectural firm. For a dozen years, into the 1980s, he drove a maroon 1951 Studebaker Champion. He does not currently own a car.

GAIL K. ELLISON is a graduate of UCLA and worked for many years on the West Coast as a photographer, designer, and writer. She is presently Writer-in-Residence at Shands HealthCare and Adjunct Faculty in the University of Florida College of Fine Arts and College of Medicine. Gail's first car was a Studebaker Silver Hawk, though eventually she transferred her automotive affection to her Porsche.

ELGIN PARK